Be EmPOWERed

How to Live Above & Beyond Life's Drama

Rasheda Kamaria Williams

Published by
Empowered Flower Girl

Be EmPOWERed
How to Live Above & Beyond Life's Drama

Library of Congress Control Number: 2016915401
ISBN: 978-0-9978800-0-7

Book Design: Tammy Monroe - Spiral Spirit Creative

Empowered Flower Girl, LLC

Printed in the United States of America

Dedication

Be EmPOWERed is dedicated to all of the girls I've met who inspired me to be my authentic (real) self.

I am truly grateful for my mother, Arzenia Williams, who always supported my dreams. She has been a loyal mother and awesome friend. I would also like to acknowledge the girls I've mentored and my mentors, Sandra Clemons and Melva Johnson.

We all can have a positive impact in someone's life. These girls and women have done that for me. I encourage everyone who reads this book to pay it forward and help someone else by listening, offering your time or simply being the wonderful person you are.

Your energy, personality and smile can brighten someone's day. The people and organizations mentioned throughout this book have contributed to my success and self-esteem.

Thank you for your support and commitment to living powerfully!

CONTENTS

Introduction

Living powerfully.

Be EmPOWERed is a tribute to the mentors and young people who inspired me throughout my life. Over the past 15 years, I have dedicated myself to supporting worthy causes, especially those that empower youth. As a child, I had many role models – from my fourth grade teacher to my Aunt Claudia – who inspired me to have faith in myself and my abilities. I wanted to do the same for others.

You may wonder what an Empowered Flower Girl is or why I chose the book title "**Be EmPOWERed**." It's actually simple.

When I was a little girl, perhaps six years old, I was asked to be a flower girl in my cousin's wedding. Less than two years later, another cousin popped the question, "Will you be our flower girl?" At seven years old, I didn't think I really had the choice. I smiled and replied, "Yes." But deep inside, I was tired of being everyone's cute little flower girl. I finally decided to take a hiatus (extended break) from active-duty family flower girl. I told my mother that I never again wanted to be a flower girl in anyone's wedding and she agreed to it. Can you believe it? I became emPOWERed at seven!

Did you notice that the word power is highlighted? This book includes "power tools" to help you in your journey into adulthood. Life isn't always easy or fair, but if you're equipped with the right tools, it makes the process more meaningful. You can learn a lot – especially from yourself.

CHAPTER 1

Live without limits.

There's no one there to stop you.

You've probably heard the old saying, "The sky is the limit." And you've probably thought to yourself, "Wow, that's a lot of space to conquer."

But I'm here to tell you that in life, there are no limits. And if there are, it's most likely that you put them there. Even the infinite (never-ending) sky can be conquered.

"Wait, what?" you probably just asked. Yes, I said it. You are the only one who limits your life. Take it from a girl who knows a thing or two about life and limitations (I'll tell you all about it in Chapter 4). I wrote this guidebook to help you become emPOWERed and create the life of your dreams. There are things we can't control, like natural disasters, who our parents are and death. But there also are many things we can control, like our attitude about life and our level of success.

We're all human and sometimes we blame others for our unhappiness. "My mom made me unhappy when she took away my cell phone and social media privileges after I stayed out past my curfew," or, "I failed my English test because I wasn't able to focus at that noisy coffee shop where my friends and I hang out and study."

I don't know if you know this or not, but your mom isn't the one who made you unhappy. She simply took away your phone and internet privileges. Perhaps you CHOSE to be unhappy. Can you believe it?

Happiness is a choice.

You could also have chosen to be understanding (you are the one who knowingly stayed out past curfew) or even happy, because now, without constant texts and notifications, you are able to study at home minus distractions, which, by the way, include those at the coffee shop.

There's a lesson to be learned from this book. What is it? I'm going to let you decide. Remember – you're reading this book because you are on the fast track to becoming emPOWERed. You have the power of choice my lady. And with the ability to choose, you can live life to its fullest.

Your parents are the wonderful folks who made it possible for you to exist and for that and that alone, you owe them a hug. You may never feel complete in life unless you have a solid relationship with your parents. I am not saying that you have to be best friends with your parents if they abandoned you, but even if they did, you owe it to yourself to forgive them. Try it and you will feel a lot better.

Power Tool # 1:

INTEGRITY

There comes a time when we must stand firm in our beliefs and accept responsibility for the choices we make and actions we take. It's called integrity and it's a noteworthy power tool.

A person who has integrity is one who will admit when she has made a mistake and will work at correcting it. A person who has integrity also will avoid making promises that she knowingly can't keep.

What would you do?

I'll give you a scenario and you decide what action should be taken:

> **While you're at the mall, you get a call from your father asking you to pick up your little brother from school at 3:30 p.m. You reply, "Sure dad. I'll do it." Unexpectedly, you see a friend and become wrapped up in conversation. You check your watch and realize that it is 4:45 p.m. What do you do?**

Sure, you can give your dad an explanation as to why you were late. But does it make up for the fact that you were over an hour late to pick up your little brother? Of course not. We all make mistakes and do things we regret from time to time. But just because we did it once or twice in the past doesn't mean that we're bad people. We've just made some poor decisions. You can learn a lot from your mistakes. You can even learn from other people's mistakes. You're only a failure if you allow yourself to become one. Be true to your word and, most of all, be true to yourself.

NOTES

CHAPTER 2

You can learn a lot from life.

Even while you're still growing.

If you live long enough, chances are there will be drama or obstacles to face. There will come a time when you'll feel alone, ashamed or even helpless. The difference between you and other girls and young women out there is that you are taking early steps to be POWERful.

If you look at where I am in my life today, you'd think that life growing up was always easy. You'd think I was always happy and had the answers to everything. Don't get me wrong, I have lots of fond childhood memories. One that comes to mind is Christmas 1986. My brother and I were overwhelmed with all of the toys and clothes we received that year. My mother worked hard to make sure I had the best Christmas ever. From a Strawberry Shortcake doll with stroller to a desk and chalkboard, I got everything I asked for and more. I mostly remember that Christmas because it's the one I spent with my older brother. It was special.

My eleventh birthday party also was particularly memorable. My best friend and I celebrated together (we were born a little over four hours apart at the same hospital). It was a backyard party that was open to the whole neighborhood. Not only did my friends show up, my brother's friends also joined in on the fun. There was a DJ, pizza and cute boys all over the place. Thinking about it makes me smile and feel warm and fuzzy inside. Life was incredible back then. No bills. No pressure. No worries. All I had to do was concentrate on my grades. That was the easy part.

Life itself was easy.
Then came middle school.

If you're reading this and you are a sixth through eighth grader, I am sure you can relate. Middle school provided its own set of challenges.

Personally, I thought I was cool. I was smart, kind of popular, fashionable and an active member in several school organizations, but I was constantly teased. Not because I was goofy or smelly or anything like that. I was teased because I got straight A's, spoke proper English, and listened to Madonna and Nirvana.

You're probably thinking, what's wrong with that? Nothing at all. But there was a group of kids in my grade who thought it was cool to skip class and be slackers. In their minds, speaking proper English was a "white thing." Although I was an African-American teenager attending a 95 percent African-American school, I was an outsider to some kids. I didn't like gangster rap. I didn't speak much slang. I was in the journalism club and competed in public speaking contests. There was no time for slacking on grammar. The kids would say mean things to me, like, "I don't like you," or, "Who do you think you are? You ain't better than us." They'd threaten to push me down the stairs. Their comments made me feel alone, like an alien on another planet. My self-esteem had been shot down numerous times.

But that all changed when I started making journal entries. One of my favorite middle school teachers, Mrs. Pattie, gave us a yearlong assignment to write in our journals daily. I wrote a detailed description of the taunting (teasing) and how it made me feel. My teacher gave me some good advice. She said that there always will be people in life who for some reason or another don't want to see you happy. They'll want to see you fail. Not necessarily because they're bad people but because they may feel threatened or insecure. Mrs. Pattie said that I had a lot of talent and that many artists, humanitarians, scholars and philosophers were ridiculed and rejected by some because they, too, were "different." She mentioned people who I aspired to be like, including Jesus Christ, Dr. Martin Luther King Jr., Mahatma Gandhi and Oprah Winfrey.

Be EmPOWERed

When she mentioned all of these incredible people, it made me feel a lot better. I thought to myself, "Wow, people had bad things to say about Jesus and he kept working miracles." Can you imagine what the world would be like today if these remarkable human beings had changed to be like everyone else? Think about it. What if Jesus took the advice of the naysayers (aka haters)? What if Dr. King gave up on his dream?

So the next time someone tells you that your idea is stupid or that you're not good enough, remember that you are the queen of the universe and you rule.

Nothing can stop you.

Power Tool # 2:

KNOWLEDGE

Knowledge is power and it is the most important power tool of them all. A wise person never knows too much. You may overeat, oversleep or go overboard, but you will never over know.

There's always something else to learn. For instance, did you know that no word in the English language rhymes with silver, purple, orange or month? Or did you know that the average American spends six months over the course of their lives waiting at red lights? You probably didn't know that you didn't know this information. That is what I believe is so cool about knowledge – it's vast and lacks an expiration date.

When you seek knowledge, you open yourself up to numerous possibilities. You can learn anything you want. If you want to be a pilot when you grow up, learn to fly an aircraft, or if you've always had a dream of becoming an oceanographer, learn more about marine biology. These simple steps can help you achieve your goals and may help you win a spot on the game show *Jeopardy*. LOL.

There's no such thing as
useless knowledge.

CHAPTER 3

Strive for your personal best.

Be EmPOWERed

Doesn't it seem like sometimes when we plan to give it our all, we just don't measure up? Or perhaps we see where we could have done better? We all have the desire to be the best. Well what about this: Instead of striving to be the absolute best in the whole world, how about being your personal best?

Come on, chica. You have to give yourself credit sometimes. You are doing a lot for your age – probably more than your parents and grandparents did.

Not only are you expected to maintain good grades at school, but you put in community service hours (especially if you're in high school) and participate in extracurricular activities like sports, band or Girl Scouts. On top of all of that, you still find time to study, post status updates, eat dinner with family and catch up with friends.

That's a lot for someone who only has 24 hours in a day, eight of which are supposed to be spent sleeping. So here is what I am saying to you – give it your all and don't beat yourself up if you don't get the highest score or the largest trophy. For example: Say you took a math test last month and got 15 out of 20 correct. The next month you take another test and score 17. But guess what? Some other kid scored 19 out of 20 and received the highest score.

I know for some of you that may be a bummer. You wanted the highest score in the class and since you didn't get it, you're feeling like less than the intelligent babe you are. Well wake up little sister because you just scored two points higher than you did on last month's test. That is a reason to celebrate and put that test in a fancy frame!

What I just explained is the concept behind achieving your personal best. I can recall the time when I was a freshman in college and had received the results from my math placement test. The highest possible score one could earn was a 40 but only a 20 was required to pass. When I opened the letter I was disappointed to see that I had only scored a 27. Crap, I thought. I was really hoping to pass with at least a 30. I didn't even acknowledge myself for exceeding the passing score. All I could think about was the fact that someone else scored higher.

In retrospect (a look at the past), I realize how often I wouldn't give myself credit for my achievements. Like you, I was doing a lot. From maintaining a 3.6 grade point average and volunteering to working a part-time job, I had a full plate. I am sure I would have been happier and achieved even more if I had celebrated my accomplishments.

Give yourself a standing ovation from time to time and reward yourself for doing YOUR best.

Don't be afraid to
be your own cheerleader.

23

CHAPTER 4

When life throws you lemons, make lemon meringue pie.

Be EmPOWERed

When it comes to making the best out of what life gives you, I've become an expert. I've been given lemons before. Lemons can be sour, bitter and tart. But you can make glorious desserts with lemons: lemon chiffon cake, lemon torte or lemon poppy seed muffins. I chose to take the lemons I received and make lemon meringue pie. Yum!

I was at a happy point of my life when I was 17 years old. I was preparing for graduation, college and a summer internship at the Detroit News, one of the city's largest daily newspapers. Life was grand. At the same time, my Aunt Claudia was diagnosed with a rare cancer. Aunt Claudia had a major impact in my life. She was intelligent, funny, strong, generous and compassionate. She was everything I wanted to be in life. She and her husband, Uncle Maddox, took me into their home when I was 13.

I never once thought Aunt Claudia would leave me, even after she started radiation and chemotherapy. Unfortunately, both were unsuccessful at removing the cancer. While I was preparing for high school graduation, Aunt Claudia got really sick. Her immune system was unable to handle the powerful side effects of chemo. I received the disappointing news that she couldn't make it to my graduation ceremony. That was a sour lemon.

I graduated in June 1997 with honors. Aunt Claudia was proud. At that moment, I felt like I had accomplished something magnificent: I made her smile. She hadn't smiled in a long time. The smiles turned upside down when a year later her doctor told us that there was nothing else that could be done to cure Aunt Claudia's disease.

In 1998, Aunt Claudia died just 21 days short of her 54th birthday. Uncle Maddox and I found her lifeless in the bedroom. I felt numb. I didn't cry for two months.

I was too busy to fall apart. When Aunt Claudia died, I was a sophomore (second-year student) in college. Dealing with her death made getting through the school year challenging. But I was determined to find light at the end of the tunnel. I applied myself 110 percent. I earned all A's the same semester Aunt Claudia passed away. It's like I transferred all of my frustration, anger and sorrow into positive energy.

I encourage you to do the same. Whenever darkness falls upon your life, remember the opposite – light. Light is powerful and it never fails to outshine darkness.

I will be honest and let you know that I wasn't always so sure about this. Two years after Aunt Claudia passed, Uncle Maddox became ill and depressed. I tried my best to care for him. But sometimes it doesn't matter how much you try; if God has a plan, you'll have to follow it.

I had gone to a dance recital in the afternoon. When I returned home that evening, I heard Uncle Maddox in his room, moaning and grunting as if he had fallen and injured himself. I rushed to the room to find him suffering in pain. He told me that he wanted to die. I tried to convince him to go the hospital, but he wanted to die. He had attempted suicide. There was nothing I could do to stop him. I was there to witness the whole thing. This time the lemon was bitter – extremely bitter.

Uncle Maddox lived a full year after the suicide attempt. He died in December 2000. I thought I would never get over that incident. But I did. Did I do it alone? No. Was I always strong and powerful? No. I made it through because of my spirit. I had a spirit of determination. I had a supportive family. And most of all, I had faith in myself.

Noteworthy Thought
There are no stupid questions.

Being powerful doesn't mean that you can't ask questions, get help or put your trust in others. The truth is we all need a little help every now and then. If you don't know the answer to a question, what do you do? No, you don't sit there quietly fearing that your question is "stupid." You ask your question with confidence.

There's another old saying that goes, "The only stupid question is the one you don't ask." I think they had it wrong. It should read, "You are the only one who thinks your question is stupid." Forget looking stupid. How could you of all people look stupid anyway? You're an intelligent young woman who folks admire. Inquisitive (question-asking and curious) folks always look smart. Think about it. The kid in your class who always raises her hand with a question is almost always the one who gets the best grades on exams. Why? She isn't afraid to ask "stupid" questions. My advice to you – ask lots questions, even the "dumb" ones.

How to make "stupid" questions smart.

Never precede (begin) your question with this statement: "I know this is a stupid question, but …" Statements like this are guaranteed to influence that person's opinion of your question. Chances are, if you tell them your question is stupid, they'll agree. Simply ask your question minus the "stupid" statement.

28

NOTES

CHAPTER 5

Discover your passion.

Discover yourself.

Be EmPOWERed

When I was a teenager, I loved to write. Writing was an escape for me. It allowed me to express myself and helped me escape all that was mundane (boring) about the day.

I loved writing poetry, speeches and short stories. I even entered some of my most brilliant works in local and statewide contests. I wrote all the time and when I entered middle school, I jumped at the chance to participate in the school's program for young journalists. We created and published – along with adult mentors – the Barbour Fresh Press. I thought it was the best school newsletter in the city. I was proud to be a part of that program.

My passion for writing didn't stop there. I signed up for a journalism course as a sophomore in high school. I wrote features about issues affecting teens. I'll never forget the column I wrote about kids being allowed to view R-rated films without parental guidance. Some friends thought it was cool but others thought it was corny. To my surprise, I earned a trophy and $50 for it.

That award-winning article helped land me a full Presidential Scholarship to attend Wayne State University's Journalism Institute for Media Diversity. I graduated in 2001 with a 3.7 grade point average. I attribute my success to my passion.

I discovered that when you put your all into a project, others appreciate what you do, and sometimes they reward you for it. But don't let the reward be your only motivation.

Do what you enjoy and do it well because you're passionate about it. Make whatever you do an art. Be expressive. Be creative. But most of all, be your true self.

How do you define your passion? Well it's different from person to person. I suggest paying close attention to the activities that you enjoy doing the most. Typically, you can find your passion in the things that make you smile inside and outside.

If your passion is writing, then go ahead and enter essay contests or volunteer to help other kids in your class improve their writing skills. And if you love to sing or act, why not join your school's or community's theatre group? I believe that you'll be a lot happier in life and will find inner peace if you involve yourself in the activities that touch, move and inspire you. Be sure to have fun along the way!

Passion and purpose are similar but there's a slight difference.
See Chapter 6 for details.

Power Tool # 3

SELF-APPRECIATION

Your parents love you. Your friends admire you. Your teachers absolutely adore you. But how do you feel about yourself? While other people may have one opinion about who you are, you may have a different view of yourself. My goal is to make sure you are practicing self-love.

I want you to do something that you normally may not do. Stand in front of a mirror and stare at yourself for two minutes. As you are gazing into the mirror, think of all the words that describe you and make you feel good inside.

Smart. Beautiful. Mature. Creative. POWERful.

Do those or similar adjectives come to mind? If not, keep staring until you find words that make you smile. Once you've found that one adjective that inspires you, become it. If beautiful feels good, then become beauty. Once you've mastered this exercise, you are on your way to becoming an expert in the area of self-appreciation. This power tool is sure to help increase your confidence and self-esteem. When you really and truly appreciate yourself, others will follow your lead.

NOTES

CHAPTER 6

What's my purpose?

The perplexing question.

Be EmPOWERed

How many times have you found yourself asking, "What is my life's purpose?" You may not have thought much about it since you're still young. But as you get older, you'll probably start to inquire (ask). Several questions are likely to arise, including: Who am I? What am I here for? What's in store for my future?

I would like to give you the answers, but the truth is, I don't have any for you. No one except you can answer these questions – not your mom, not your dad, not your teacher. Trust me when I tell you that the answers probably won't come to you for several years. In addition, your responses may change three or four times before you've reached a final conclusion.

When I was in the fourth grade, I decided that my purpose in life was to go to college and study ecology. I was convinced that I would save the planet by becoming an environmental scientist. I even started conducting research on careers in ecology. Can you believe it? How someone starts out wanting to be an environmentalist and ends up being an author and journalist is wild, in my opinion.

But it's all part of the growing process.

You may change your mind a hundred times or more about your career interests, religious and spiritual beliefs, or hobbies. It's perfectly normal to be undecided. After elementary school, I decided that ecology wasn't for me. I came up with the idea of being on television as a reporter or talk show host. I thought I discovered my ultimate career!

Well things changed again after high school. By the time I was well into my sophomore year in college, I decided that I no longer wanted to be a television news reporter. At first I was excited by the thought of appearing in front of millions of viewers to announce breaking news and information. Television reporting seemed like the perfect choice for me, but something changed. I started tutoring kids in English and writing. It was a part-time hobby at first, but it became more than that after a while. I felt like I was making a difference.

That single volunteer experience inspired me to continue giving back to the community. I became a mentor and volunteer for a wonderful organization in Detroit called Alternatives for Girls (AFG). I was assigned three girls to mentor. I took the girls to museums, dance recitals, and so many other fun and educational places. We had an awesome time together and learned a lot from each other. As a matter of fact, I am still an active volunteer with AFG. My experience in the community helped me realize my purpose. Some people say they find their purpose speaking with God. Others have discovered it while dreaming. I attribute my life's purpose to God (also known as The Creator). It is my belief that The Creator guided me to the various organizations that, in turn, inspired me to take on community service as my motivation for living POWERfully.

If you don't fully understand this concept, that's okay. Take notes and be sure to refer to this chapter in the future when the subject comes up with a career counselor at school or during a one-on-one session with a life coach, for instance. Remember not to feel frustrated, embarrassed or less than intelligent because you are unsure of what high school or college you want to attend or what it is that you want to do when you grow up. Figuring out the answers to these questions is all a part of growing up. Keep an open mind and keep dreaming.

Noteworthy Thought
Don't compare yourself to a celebrity.

Beauty fades. Trends become passé (old or out of style). Material things lose their value. So what's left? I ask because I think it is important that as young women, we understand the value of looking beyond the physical. It's easier said than done, I know.

You and I both know how much of a challenge it can be to keep a positive self-image, especially when we live in a world where image is everything. We see gorgeous, long-haired, large-breasted women in videos and on the cover of popular magazines. It makes us feel self-conscious sometimes. But I am here to let you in on a little secret. They get paid to look beautiful. Seriously.

Imagine that you are a mega pop star. You probably have an annual salary of more than a million dollars, which includes royalties, endorsement deals and paid appearances. Now imagine that you have a personal trainer, chef and yoga instructor to help you along the way seven days a week. With all of that help, you're guaranteed to look red carpet ready!

Keeping it 100.

The reality is, you are not a pop star. Not saying that you can't be one, you just aren't right now. If you had millions of dollars, you would probably look and live like a celebrity too. So save yourself the grief and stop worrying about how to look like a video vixen.

NOTES

CHAPTER 7

You can be the change this world needs.

Be EmPOWERed

There are so many things that the world needs. One of the most important things is you. You have the ability to make the world a better place. Sure, you're young and not yet eligible to run for president, but politicians aren't the only folks who make a difference. If you have the desire, I encourage you to run for office when you're old enough. For now, understand that you can make an important contribution to this planet even as a teenager.

When I was a child, I heard adults say things like, "Children should be seen and not heard." Get real! You have the power to make this world a better place, and all it takes is the courage to speak up for yourself and your community. If you are passionate about an issue, don't be afraid to speak up and take action. I learned that even adults are afraid to speak their minds for fear of looking stupid or upsetting others. Sometimes it takes a little discomfort to get an issue resolved.

For instance: Say you have a friend who drinks alcohol even though she is only 15. She asks you to take a walk with her to the store for beer. Your friend, who looks a lot older than her age, frequently purchases alcoholic beverages from the store without ever being asked for an ID. If you're like me, then you'd feel uncomfortable hanging out with someone who is breaking the law. So what would you do? Would you be too afraid to tell your friend how uncomfortable you were feeling. Would you insult your friend and tell her that she is an irresponsible jerk? Or would you get the name and location of the store that was selling alcohol to kids and report it to the police?

It's a tough decision to make, right? Trust me when I tell you that you'll be faced with tough choices throughout your entire life. The solution to problems will not always be easy and sometimes issues will not always be resolved. But remember to always maintain your integrity. Polonius a character in Shakespeare's *Hamlet* said, "To thine own self be true."

In the case of underage drinking, I should let you know that it is illegal. It is against the law for adults to purchase alcohol for minors (people under the legal drinking age). Have you thought about what you'd do? If you don't want to ruin your friendship by insulting your friend, I suggest not judging her. Telling her that she is an idiot or a loser probably will make the situation worse. She may be less offended and more likely to respect your views if you told her how her behavior made you feel. "I feel" statements can make a world of difference in your relationships with others.

Here is an example:

YOU: *"Hey (insert friend's name), you're my friend and I really care about you, but when you (insert behavior), it makes me feel (insert emotion)."*

FRIEND: *"I never knew you felt that way. Thanks for being honest. I apologize if I upset you. I won't ask you to do it again."*

The above scenario is ideal and things may not go as well for you and your friend. Don't get bummed out over it. A true friend will consider your feelings, too, and not end your friendship over a situation like this. You also have the option of anonymously (without anyone knowing who you are) contacting your local police department to report the store whose employees are engaging in illegal activity. This takes courage, but in the end you'll be making a difference in your community and in the lives of those you love (like your friend).

The power of one.

I once heard a friend say, "I'm just one person. I can't make a difference." Have you ever heard someone say that? Have you said it?

Sometimes we all feel like there is nothing we can do to make the world a better, happier place. After all, the world is gigantic. I did a little research and found out that the earth's circumference (distance around a circle measured from the diameter using the mathematical formula $[C = \Pi x D]$) at the equator is about 25,000 miles. In addition, there are 7 billion people on the planet.

So you might say to yourself: "That's a lot of people. How in the world am I going to change things?"

The answer is simple. Say for instance you and nine of your friends from school decide to raise money for a homeless shelter in your community. If each of you went out and collected $50, then the homeless shelter would receive a $500 donation. That is enough money to buy food for 100 people to eat for one day! Now imagine that you and all of your friends had said, "Let's not do this because we can't make a difference."

If each of you had that attitude, then there would be 100 people out there without food for a day. There are 24 hours in a day. That is a lot of time to go without food. Do you understand where I'm going with this?

Let me explain.

When each individual decides to take action, that is one more person who can help. In the example I used, you – the individual – raised $50. If you hadn't participated, then the group would have been $50 short. That means that 10 people would go hungry that day. Now are you beginning to see how you – as one person – can make a difference?

You can!

Think about things you can do to help others – perhaps those in your family, your city, the country or the world. Do you really like animals? If so, ask your parents to help you find an animal shelter where you can volunteer. Are you passionate about the environment? Talk to your teacher about starting a garden or recycling program at school. There are so many things you can do to be the change.

For the Change in Action activity on page 49, you have the opportunity to brainstorm ways to make a difference. Take time to write down the things that inspire you and research how you can contribute to the cause through volunteering. Good luck.

NOTES

Change in action

What I care about	Volunteer opportunity

Noteworthy Thought
Be the change.

When the world seems lonely and no one appears to care,

BE COMFORT.

When there's darkness in every corner and your vision is blurry,

BE LIGHT.

When you're surrounded by hate and fear is present,

BE LOVE.

When others are depressed and hope is an illusion,

BE JOY.

When you can no longer bear the weight of the world, don't give up;

BE UNSTOPPABLE.

By Rasheda Kamaria Williams

This poem was inspired by Mahatma Gandhi, who believed that

We must be the change we wish to see in this world.

CHAPTER 8

Reach beyond the stars.

The galaxy is yours to explore.

Be EmPOWERed

Never let fear keep you from flying. You were meant to soar beyond the clouds. Remember that you are the only person who has control over your future. In fact, the future doesn't even exist right now.

We are in the present. My advice is to plan for tomorrow but live for today. Today you probably feel like you can do anything. You probably have an I-can attitude about life – at least I hope so after having read this book. Please keep this attitude as you move into the future. I hope you haven't forgotten that the world needs you. I know that's a lot of pressure, but it's true.

The world needs strong, fearless girls and women to be leaders. The world can use more role models, mentors and teachers. I am confident that you are one of those who will be POWERful. You already are.

You are in a unique position, young lady. There's no one else out there like you. You are a perfect creation because The Creator makes no mistakes. I am not a psychic but I am willing to bet that you have friends or family who look up to you. They often brag to others about your talent, intelligence and fierceness. Those characteristics will take you far but only if you let them.

Recite the Empowered Flower Girl Oath frequently for a little extra power.

What's this? The Empowered Flower Girl Oath (found in the next section) states that girls and young women should always "aspire to live POWERfully." Sounds familiar, doesn't it? Of course; it's in the title of this book. I chose it as the title because I want you to remember it for the rest of your life.

When you live without limits, you open yourself up to greatness. Imagine how far you can go if you never fear flying. Now get out there and explore the galaxy!

Words to live by.

I know your parents or school librarian may have instilled in you certain morals and rules that are golden. One of them probably is to never rip the pages out of a book.

Today you can tell your parents that it's okay. I, Rasheda Kamaria Williams, encourage you to tear out this page and post it on your wall, or in your school locker or even share it on social media.

Why? Because these are words to live by, and while you don't have to recite them aloud every day, be conscious (aware) of their power. Be open to this message.

The Empowered Flower Girl Oath

I am the *epitome* of love;
I possess unlimited potential.
I am the *essence* of life;
My being is essential.

I have the ability to change the world;
There's nothing I can't be.
I am filled with greatness;
And I choose to live powerfully.

By Rasheda Kamaria Williams

Definitions

epitome: a perfect example : an example that represents or expresses something very well.
essence: the nature of something : the qualities that make a thing what it is.

POWER survey

It's time to take a look at your personal power. This is not one of those surveys that gives you points for right answers and makes judgments based on your score. It is designed to help you become aware of your power and push you to be POWERful in every area of your life.

1. In your own words, describe what it means to live POWERfully:

2. What steps can you take in your life today to make you more POWERful in the future?

3. Name three women in history who you think are POWERful and explain why:

4. Describe something POWERful you've done to help someone else:

NOTES

Subject reference

Noteworthy people, places and things mentioned in this book

About the author
Rasheda Kamaria Williams

RELEVANT. RELATABLE. REAL.

Rasheda Kamaria Williams is the founder and chief empowering officer for Empowered Flower Girl. She is a communications professional, mentor and speaker with a passion for community service.

She holds a bachelor of arts degree in journalism from Wayne State University and is a graduate of Cass Technical High School in Detroit.

For more than a decade, Rasheda has been committed to making a difference in the lives of women and children. Since 2001, she has mentored a total of seven girls ages 5 to 19.

She has earned numerous awards for her dedication to community service and social change.

A survivor of bullying, Rasheda was featured in the May 2011 issue of *Cosmopolitan* magazine in the article, "Being Bullied Changed My Life." Her journey from excluded to empowered motivated her to launch Empowered Flower Girl in 2010.

Connect with Rasheda

Email: **rkamaria@empoweredflowergirl.com**
Twitter: **efgempowered**
Facebook & Instagram: **empoweredflowergirl**

About Empowered Flower Girl

Rooted in diversity, inclusion and inspiration, Empowered Flower Girl is a social enterprise on a mission to transform the way young people related to one another.

The company partners with schools, communities and families seeking solutions to cyberbullying, drama, relational aggression, and other social and communication challenges facing middle and high school students.

Founded in 2010 by Rasheda Kamaria Williams, Empowered Flower Girl offers engaging and inspiring workshops and programs for youth and adults designed to increase confidence, self-esteem, empathy and altruism.

Learn more at
empoweredflowergirl.com
#BeEmpowered

Made in the USA
Monee, IL
05 April 2021

63712602R00037